Original title:
Lace and Leather

Copyright © 2025 Creative Arts Management OÜ
All rights reserved.

Author: Tobias Winslow
ISBN HARDBACK: 978-1-80586-073-0
ISBN PAPERBACK: 978-1-80586-545-2

Timeless Compositions

In a closet filled with flair,
Where costumes dance with glee,
A corset whispers secrets,
And pants roll out for tea.

The boots, they tap a beat,
As if they know the score,
A whimsy in the fabric,
Bringing laughter to the door.

Textured Emotions

A jacket hugs with style tight,
Like friends who never leave,
With pockets full of giggles,
And zippers that deceive.

The gloves, they wave hello,
In a manner cheeky, bold,
Each fabric tells a story,
With threads of joy, retold.

The Narrative of Fabric

The skirt twirls 'round with flair,
A fable in the breeze,
While top hats give a wink,
Causing quite the tease.

The ties they sway with jest,
As colors clash and play,
In patterns that combine,
To turn the dull to gay.

Fathoms of Feeling

A vest that hums a tune,
Remembering the past,
While collars raise a brow,
And make the moments last.

Each stitch a chuckle shared,
In the grand parade of fate,
Where whimsy finds a haven,
And every thread's first-rate.

Dark Threads and Light

In shadows where giggles find their pace,
A dance between soft and a daring trace.
Silk whispers and winks in dim twilight,
While humor prances, a playful delight.

Jokes stitched with mischief, oh what a pair,
Tangles of fun, like wild, tousled hair.
A sly wink here, a nudge on the side,
In the game of charm, we both take pride.

The Duality of Allure

A velvet touch plays tricks on the mind,
With each little tease, chaos intertwined.
Sweet smiles hide secrets, a giggle or two,
It's all in good jest, as jesters pursue.

A wink and a nod, oh, what could be next?
Surprises abound, like a cheeky text.
Dual tones collide, a twist to the tease,
With laughter resounding, we play as we please.

Intricate Patterns of Desire

Patterns that tangle, a quirky embrace,
Where laughter erupts, joining the chase.
Delicate tickles and playful jeers,
In this web of winks, we conquer our fears.

A pause for a pun, then back to the fray,
Like curves in the night, we twist and sway.
The art of seduction, a snicker, a spin,
In this dance of delight, we both can win.

Touchstones of Temptation

A teasing glance sends shivers with glee,
We're tangled in whims, just you and me.
In a world of giggles, we shuffle and sway,
With a sly little grin, we playfully play.

Each jest is a treasure, an alluring tease,
Binding us tighter, like mischievous bees.
With humor our armor, we boldly tread,
In the realm of laughter, where no one dreads.

The Dance of Resilience

In a club full of quirky attire,
People twirl, never seem to tire.
Laughing shoes click on the floor,
A slip or two? It's just folklore.

Bouncing back from each little trip,
They embrace the groove, feel the rip.
Who knew that flailing could be art?
A wobbly dance can warm the heart.

Threads of Longing

A stitch in time may save some falls,
But frayed edges make the best calls.
Invisible threads pull them near,
Each twirl an echo of cheer.

A longing glance, mischief in play,
Stitching moments that won't fray.
A snag here, a knot there,
Laughter bursts, filling the air.

Seductive Embroidery

With patterns bold and colors bright,
Who knew the night could feel so right?
A wink and nod, what a tease,
Flirtatious threads that aim to please.

Spinning tales with every twine,
Entwined in mischief, oh so fine.
Giggles split the midnight air,
Entangled hearts caught unaware.

Hidden Revelations

Beneath the fabric, secrets hide,
Jokes and jests, they won't abide.
A playful whisper in the seams,
Life's quirks wrap around our dreams.

Unraveled threads in the moonlight,
Make the trivial feel just right.
In laughter's loop, we find the truth,
Hidden treasures of eternal youth.

Patterns of Passion

In a world of threads, we dance so bold,
Twirling in garments, stories unfold.
We wear our quirks with giggles so loud,
In patterns of mischief, we feel so proud.

Hats tipped just right, a wink in our eyes,
With each little outfit, we always surprise.
Stitching our laughter, a tapestry spun,
In this playful world, we always have fun.

Beneath the Surface

Underneath it all, secret smiles peek,
With sighs of humor, we flirt and we speak.
Whispers of nonsense, yet oh-so sincere,
In our cozy corners, we have no fear.

Patterns entwined, like jokes in the air,
Beneath the surface, we lighten despair.
We dance on the edge of a cheeky delight,
In this wild fabric, we shimmer so bright.

Emblem of Enchantment

With winks and nods, we play our own game,
Wearing our grins, we're never the same.
An emblem of fun, made just for the night,
In a swirl of colors, we take to flight.

Dancing in circles, we giggle and sway,
As echoes of laughter come out to play.
The world is our canvas, bright and sublime,
In this fabric of joy, we laugh every time.

The Fabric of Longing

In threads of desire, we weave a jest,
With a wink and a nod, we know we're the best.
Longing for laughter, we twirl and we spin,
In a whimsical dance, let the fun begin.

Happiness stitched into every seam,
In the fabric of life, we laugh and we dream.
So here's to our bond, stitched tight with cheer,
In this playful tapestry, we hold each other dear.

Embrace of Grit and Grace

In a world where rubber meets the road,
Gritty pants and a spicy code.
With every shimmy, there's a wink,
Laughing stitches as we rethink.

A brazen belt in a dance class,
Daring folks to trip and pass.
Twisted seams and giggles free,
Everyone joins the jubilee.

When the day's done, we let them sway,
In silly outfits, come what may.
Swirling skirts and cheeky charms,
Invite the night to lose its qualms.

In the end, it's all in jest,
Where twisted threads are truly best.
So grab a friend, now have no fear,
In this rough and ready atmosphere!

A Stitch in the Night

Under stars, where darkness sings,
Threads glimmer like mischievous wings.
Purls and twirls in a moonlit dance,
Crafting mischief without a chance.

Needles click, a rhythm loud,
Turning heads in a giggling crowd.
Whispers of fabrics made to tease,
Winks exchanged in the evening breeze.

With patches stitched, we drolly prance,
Each turn brings cheeky circumstance.
Beneath the glow, we raise a toast,
To sharp designs we love the most.

Upon the fabric of this night,
We weave a tale of pure delight.
For in this whimsy, we unite,
Crafty souls in laughter's light!

Veils of Texture

Layers of fabric, soft and thick,
Draped like secrets in a flick.
Swirls and patterns that make us grin,
Each twist and turn, let the fun begin.

The ruffles bounce with every jest,
Some miss the mark, but that's the quest.
A fabric war, with colors bright,
Laughing louder with every sight.

In every thread, a tale unfolds,
Of clumsy dancers, antics bold.
The twists of texture keep us spun,
In silly games, we laugh and run.

Veils of merriment, catch the sights,
Hiding giggles from the nights.
For in this tapestry we'll stay,
Sowing joy in a playful fray!

Chasing Echoes in Dark Fabric

Through shadows cast by midnight flair,
We prance about without a care.
Echoes giggle, weaving dreams,
Beneath a moon that softly beams.

Hidden secrets in pockets deep,
Where laughter lingers and never sleeps.
Woven jokes bring merry cheer,
Draped in fabric, we disappear.

Chasing shadows, we twist and sway,
Frayed edges won't keep us at bay.
The fabric bends, with every jest,
In this playful beat, we feel the best.

As echoes flit through darkened seams,
We'll stitch together the silliest themes.
In textured tales, we find our glee,
In cozy corners, just you and me!

Echoes in Embroidery

In a patch of dreams that twirl and spin,
Threads of laughter peek and grin.
Stitching secrets, wild and sly,
A funny dance, just you and I.

Frogs in bow ties, cats in skirts,
Twisting patterns, oh, it flirts.
What's that sparkle in your eye?
A tangle of fun that's flying high.

Woven Whispers

A fabric's tale, the giggles grow,
Twirling tales that barely show.
With every knot, a chuckle hides,
In gentle fibers, joy abides.

Confetti dreams and polka dots,
Witty winks and silly knots.
Every thread, a jest to share,
In this fabric world, we dance with flair.

The Art of Restraint

Funny rules in a silken game,
Tied up tight, yet never tame.
A wink, a nudge, a playful sigh,
In the art of holding dreams awry.

Tangled chords and whip-smart puns,
We play it cool, just us two funs.
Though bound by fabric, we run free,
In laughter's thread, there's no decree.

Shades of Temptation

A dash of color, a hint of tease,
Fabric flirtations aimed to please.
With every shade, a playful mix,
Wrapped in laughter, our funny tricks.

Velvet whispers, playful spins,
A parade of quirks, where charm begins.
In soft embraces, we find delight,
Shadows of humor bask in the light.

Mysterious Layers Unfolding

Under wraps of twinkling flair,
Curious whispers fill the air.
Each unravel leaves us amazed,
What a sight, so warmly praised.

A playful twist, a wink, a grin,
Secrets hiding deep within.
Jokes are stitched in every seam,
Crafty tales that tease and gleam.

Waltzing on this fabric dance,
Funky patterns in a chance.
Giggles hop with every fold,
Mischief wrapped, but never cold.

Oh, the tales these threads could tell,
In every swirl, there lies a spell.
Fun awaits in every place,
Layers thick, yet light with grace.

Boundaries of Softness and Strength

Fuzzy hugs in sturdy guise,
Toughness hidden, like a prize.
With a wink and cheeky cheer,
Strength in softness, oh so dear.

Daring moves in playful style,
Witty banter makes us smile.
Beneath the tough, a soft embrace,
Who knew strength could have such grace?

Tickled pink by every twist,
In this game, you can't resist.
Bold and tame in one sweet breath,
Life's a blend of fun and stealth.

Like a puppy's playful bite,
Rough around, yet soft at night.
Boundaries blur, a funny dance,
Living life with every chance.

Enigmas in Every Stitch

Silly secrets tied and knotted,
Who would guess? Oh, not you, you nodded.
Patterns hide a funny tale,
Weaving laughter without fail.

In the corners, quirky dots,
Each connection hits the spot.
Jokes are lurking, oh so sly,
In a garment, dreams can fly.

Buttons giggle, zippers tease,
Each reveal brings joy and ease.
A silly twist, an odd delight,
Finding smiles wrapped up tight.

Every curve a playful spree,
Crafting shapes so whimsically.
Unravel tales, embrace the fun,
In every stitch, there's joy to run.

Handcrafted Whispers in the Dark

A stitch of giggles in the night,
Where subtle sparks ignite delight.
In corners where the shadows play,
We dance our worries far away.

A cheeky grin, a sly remark,
As secrets twirl in twilight's spark.
With playful whispers in the air,
We turn the mundane into a dare.

The fabric bends, yet does not break,
We juggle dreams with every shake.
In threads of mischief we entwine,
Creating laughter, oh so fine.

So let's embrace the whimsical,
In midnight's dance, so typical.
With every twist and turn we find,
A joy that echoes, intertwined.

The Art of Comfortable Dissonance

A riot of colors amid the black,
Each pattern laughs, no need to track.
In chaos lies a subtle grace,
We find our rhythm, out of place.

A clash of textures, bold and brash,
In every movement, we make a splash.
We giggle at the tangled mess,
Where joy and folly coalesce.

Worn-out shoes, a jaunty jump,
In this ensemble, take a bump.
With every twirl, the world's a stage,
We scribble joy on each old page.

So dance and leap, embrace the sound,
In sweet discord, our hearts unbound.
For in the art of comical strife,
We stitch together a merry life.

Classes of Shadow and Light

In a hallway where colors collide,
Dressed in things we can't decide.
Each choice is chaotic, yet so right,
An elegance in the oddest sight.

A wink of blue against the gray,
Socks with polka dots lead the way.
In every misstep, laughter's found,
In the play of hues, we're tightly wound.

A whisper here, a flash of fun,
Unequal pairs, we are not done.
Through serious doubt, we still ignite,
The classes of shadow and silly light.

So join the dance, embrace the mix,
We'll toast to style and playful tricks.
With every outfit, come what may,
We'll laugh our worries far away.

Sensations of Two Worlds

A tickle in the heart of night,
With mismatched shoes, we feel just right.
Through tangled paths of giggling glee,
We jump between reality.

The whispers of silk brush against the skin,
While rugged charm wraps in a spin.
In contrast bright, we find our cheer,
A ballet of chaos, our joy sincere.

With every glance, the world collides,
In giggles shared, our laughter guides.
From soft to tough, we twirl and sway,
In this waltz of oddities, come what may.

So let's toast to the thrill of play,
In sensations where funny leads the way.
Together we'll dance, just you and I,
In the embrace of both worlds, we'll fly.

Embracing Contrasts

In a world of fluff and grit,
She dances like a quirky fit.
Stripes and polka dots collide,
A fashion ride without a guide.

Fuzzy socks with shiny boots,
Mixing styles like funny scoots.
A tutu paired with a denim vest,
In her closet, it's a fashion fest.

High heels clack on the grass,
Prancing with style, oh what a class!
A rebel with a twinkling smile,
She strolls in boldly, packing her style.

With mismatched colors that don't blend,
She twirls around, a stylish trend.
Who cares if it's wrong or right?
Her outfit's giggles, a pure delight!

Silken Secrets

Whispers of a smooth delight,
Draped in charms that feel just right.
Satin dreams on a playful spree,
Tickling thoughts like giggling glee.

Softest touch meets a cheeky grin,
Winks exchanged in a playful spin.
A twirl in shadows, a burst of cheer,
Secret smiles that spark sincere.

With playful bows tied up with thread,
Fashion teasing with each step ahead.
Balancing style, oh what a scene,
Like a cat in a ball of green.

Hues of mischief, glinting bright,
Daring in day, charming by night.
A slip, a slide, oh what a find,
In a world so whimsically unconfined!

Bound in Elegance

Wrapped up tightly with a twist,
Fashion statements that can't be missed.
Cinch and cinch, oh what a play,
Twists of charm brighten the day.

With bows and belts and zippers too,
Creating laughs in every hue.
Swaying gently in a stylish bind,
Elegance with a wink, oh so kind.

Glittering sparks in a daring dance,
Strutting bold, oh isn't it a chance?
Every step a giggle, every turn a peek,
In the festivities, the fun is unique.

Finesse and flair, a joyful show,
Mismatched elegance, like rivers flow.
Bound by laughter, stylish and grand,
This world of whimsical, hand in hand!

The Edge of Sensation

Twirling on the cusp of fun,
A quirky mix, where worlds are spun.
Frills and thrills, a dazzling sight,
Strutting bold, embracing the night.

Crafted quirks in a fashion dream,
Mirror lights and a playful gleam.
With every step, the laughter grows,
A catwalk filled with silly bows.

Daring patterns flirt and jest,
Crinkling fortunes in every quest.
Chasing whims on a zestful spree,
A carnival of joy, just wait and see.

On the edge where giggles bloom,
Wear the wild with a splash of plume.
Sensation reigns in a playful flair,
Join the dance, a joyous affair!

The Tantalizing Tapestry

In a world of threads so bold,
Patterns weave tales, truth be told.
A stitch here, a twist over there,
Fabrics dance without a care.

Buttons giggle, zippers play,
Join the fun—don't delay!
With every pull, a cheeky grin,
Who knew fabric could cause such sin?

Colors clash, like friends at a bar,
One wants quiet, the other—ajar.
Who knew threads could be so loud?
Crafty fabric, you've drawn a crowd!

Wrap me in mischief's embrace,
In this funny fabric space!
Where materials laugh and tease,
And leave us all with giggly wheeze.

Fluid Threads of Connection

Strings of chaos intertwine,
Patterns form, oh so fine!
Each loop and knot is quite the sight,
Sewn with laughter, stitched with delight.

My sweater's got a mind of its own,
It stretches wide, then feels like a drone!
When cuddled up, it starts to joke,
Bantering back like a funny bloke!

I wore a belt that danced all day,
It wiggled and giggled—such a display!
Every buckle's a mood, what a game,
My wardrobe's gone wild, oh what a shame!

But who can resist such playful threads?
Each garment speaks, even when it treads.
Wrapped in humor, so snug and bright,
A wardrobe of giggles, oh what a sight!

Journey Through Stitches

Step right up, it's quite a ride,
Through seams and stitches, come decide!
A patchwork quilt of joy and glee,
Each square tells tales, come join me!

From an ankle sock that likes to dance,
To a cap that flirts at first glance.
Every thread whispers comical tunes,
While hems waltz under the silvery moons.

Oh, the pockets filled with giggle-fits,
Each holds secrets, oh what a blitz!
A hat with a joke—a real knee-slapper,
Join in the fun, it loves to yapper!

So heed this trip through fabric land,
Where every garment lends a hand.
Stitched with laughter, wrapped with cheer,
In this funny journey—bring your beer!

Echoes of Enticement

Hear the whispers of playful seams,
In the fabric jungle, nothing's as it seems.
Tassels tease and buttons prance,
A funny tale in every chance.

With pockets deep like hidden quests,
What treasures lie? Just take some rests!
A pen, a snack, maybe a snail,
This attire loves to tell a tale!

The colors clash like rascally kids,
Who knew a fabric could wear such bids?
Laughter ripples like a soft caress,
In this whimsical thread, we're all a mess!

So wrap yourself in comical threads,
Where every giggle stitches and spreads.
In this attire, oh how you'll glow,
A tapestry of laughter—row by row!

The Dance of Intertwined Hearts

In the corner of the room, they sway,
Two blurred souls lost in the fray.
One's all fluff, with bows and a twirl,
The other's got edge, ready to whirl.

A silly twist and a happy spin,
Giggles erupt, where do we begin?
With faux bravado, they strut and prance,
Every little slip sparks a wild romance.

Dresses ruffle, jackets squeak,
Both tease each other, a playful freak.
Caught in a tangle, they're quite the sight,
Hearts in stitches, day turns to night.

At the end of the song, they breathe in sync,
Sipping on joy, while winking with a wink.
Who knew two styles could make such a spark?
A punchline perfect, igniting the dark.

Threads Through Time

Once upon a time, a tassel was king,
With an attitude strong, it began to sing.
A fabric so bold met a soft silken hue,
Their flirtation ignited, and trouble just grew.

Oh the stories they spun, with zany threads,
Bickering over which wore more spreads.
One felt so fancy, the other quite tough,
They laughed at each other, but still called it love.

Through wild parties and mismatched galas,
They tangled their way through laughter and balas.
Worn down and crinkled from all of the fun,
Trendsetters together, their journey's begun.

Old patterns revive with a whimsical grin,
What once felt like chaos, now brings in a win.
Time may have passed, but they're still in style,
A patchwork of memories that always beguile.

The Language of Texture

Whispers of fabric in the sunlit air,
A curious mix that makes people stare.
With every touch, a secret's revealed,
The story of texture, and amusement concealed.

One's got sheen, the other, a plaid,
They poke and they prod, just to make Dad mad.
A game of compare, who's softer, who's bright?
Mismatched companions, what a silly sight!

In the world of fabric, they jest and they play,
Never a dull moment, come what may.
Vibrant debates on who wears it best,
This quirky duo, forever a jest.

As sun goes down, their charm stays bright,
Creating a fashion that's light and polite.
Both share a giggle amidst countless swirls,
Threads of laughter wrapped round the worlds.

Palette of Passion

With a brushstroke here and a dash of flair,
They color the night with a cheeky stare.
One's all flamboyant, a riotous tease,
The other, a contrast that brings one to knees.

In shades of ruckus, they swirl and they frown,
A canvas of chaos, they own this town.
Onlookers laugh, as colors collide,
This playful duet, with pride, they abide.

Through splatters and drips, they find their own groove,
The rhythm of patterns that always improve.
A palette so vivid makes spirits glow,
In a world of drab, they steal the show.

As laughter echoes and the night runs deep,
Their artistry blooms in the joy that they keep.
A masterpiece captured, all silly and bright,
In the dance of the bold, they twirl through the night.

Ties that Bind: A Duality

In a world of frills and flair,
Where charm meets mischievous dare,
A wink, a nudge, a playful tease,
Dress it up, or let it please.

With threads that twine and patterns bold,
The stories of shenanigans unfold.
One minute sweet, the next austere,
What's hidden beneath? Let's have a beer!

A gentle knot, a playful bind,
Contradictions are well-defined,
With every twist, life takes a spin,
Unveil the fun that lies within.

So raise a glass, let laughter flow,
In this realm of high and low,
For every stitch, a different fate,
Life's duality is up for debate!

Secrets Beneath the Surface

Underneath a calm facade,
Bubbles laughter, not so hard,
Quirky secrets tucked away,
In this game of hide and play!

Patterns clash, and colors fight,
What's wrong can turn to right,
Whispers echo, tickles tease,
In the silence, giggles freeze.

Adventures hide where eyes can't see,
A cheeky grin, a cup of tea,
With every glance, a cheeky pry,
What's the truth? Just pass me by!

So take a chance, reveal your wild,
The quiet joys of the inner child,
In the fabric of life, let's sow,
Secrets can sparkle, don't you know?

The Allure of Contrast

In the dance of soft and hard,
Life's a game, we're all a card,
A frilly edge meets sharp intent,
In this blend, I find content.

The rough and tumble, oh, what a sight,
With elegance that takes a flight,
A wink from roughness, charm on high,
Nature's jest, it catches the eye.

Fabric's friendly tug and pull,
With every twist, it's playful, full,
The beauty rests in what we wear,
In moments shared, let down your hair!

So let's embrace this playful range,
For every turn, there's room for change,
In the contrast, laughter's found,
As joy in life spins all around!

Threads of Passion and Resilience

Woven strong with tear and glee,
A tapestry of irony,
Each knot reveals a tale of old,
Unraveled dreams so bold and bold!

Through the fray, it finds its way,
Defying norms, come what may,
With laughter echoing through the seams,
Passion purls through all our dreams.

A playful tug, a gentle sway,
In every color, bright and gray,
The threads of life, they twist and twine,
With humor sweet, they boldly shine.

So laugh along, resilient hearts,
For every day, a brand new start,
In this weave, we laugh and play,
Oh, the joy in every fray!

Threads of Seduction

In a closet, secrets play,
Silk and charms in bright display.
Tickles here and tugging there,
Winks and giggles fill the air.

A little slip, a playful tease,
Caution thrown to the summer breeze.
Knot a bow, a playful fray,
Making mischief every day.

Colors clash, a wild sight,
With a wink, we dare the night.
A spin, a shimmy, oh what fun!
Every spin, a secret spun.

The thread that binds, a smile wide,
In our laughter, we confide.
Stitching dreams with every glance,
Join our merry, crazy dance.

Whispers of the Night

When twilight falls and shadows blend,
A sultry breeze, the night's best friend.
Whispers float on velvet hues,
Mischief stirs, what shall we choose?

A tickle here, a playful gaze,
Underneath the stars ablaze.
With every laugh, the world seems bright,
Entwined in giggles… oh, what a night!

Mysteries twirl as the moonlight glows,
In delightful chaos, the tension grows.
Teasing threads weave and sway,
Crafting tales in their own way.

The clock ticks on with no regret,
Each moment wrapped, a playful bet.
In the night's embrace, we'll remain,
Finding joy in every gain.

The Dance of Textures

A canvas mixed, a wild affair,
Smooth and rough, we twine with flair.
Bumps and ridges, on our way,
A tactile tale in bright array.

Satin soft invites a spin,
Brass and buckles, let's begin!
Every movement tells a story,
In our jig of playful glory.

Threads entwined, we laugh and leap,
In this mosaic, secrets keep.
With every twist, a spark ignites,
In a whirlwind of playful nights.

Colors clash, and patterns tease,
In this dance, we move with ease.
A joyful romp, unbound and free,
Textures whispering, "Come dance with me!"

Shadows and Stitches

In the dark, we scribble fun,
Making shadows dance and run.
With stitches pulled and knots undone,
We weave a tale 'til we see the sun.

Stuck on a whim, we lost control,
Fabric and laughter, they take their toll.
Twirling fabrics in a bright display,
Get ready for our wild ballet!

Secrets fumble in a playful bind,
With every tug, a laugh we find.
A patterned mess, a charming sight,
In every corner, pure delight.

So grab a thread, let's tie a knot,
In shadows deep, we'll hit the spot.
A patchwork of moments, stitched so tight,
We embrace the joy of our playful night.

The Weave of Attraction.

In a world where threads collide,
A quirky dance they can't abide.
With a wink and a playful spin,
They tangle up, let the fun begin!

Gossamer dreams and stitches bold,
Crafting laughter, stories told.
One caught on a whimsical seam,
Now they're stuck in a fashion dream!

Twisted ribbons, a tangled plight,
Fumbling fortunes, oh what a sight!
Fabrics flirt, they twist and sway,
In this merry game, who'll win the day?

A splash of color, a dash of flair,
In this zany courtship, there's love in the air.
With giggles and snaps, let's not forget,
This joyous bond we won't regret!

Whispers of Soft Threads

Silken whispers tease the night,
Threads giggle in their playful flight.
At every turn, a ticklish jest,
Crafting smiles, it's for the best!

A knot tied up with giggly squeals,
In tangled stories, the joy reveals.
Beneath the surface, soft and sweet,
Their charming chats skip a beat!

Frayed edges bring their own delight,
A snickering glimmer in the twilight.
Twists and turns, they jest with glee,
In this fabric world, let it be free!

Fables spun from needle's dance,
With every stitch, they take a chance.
Side by side in this twined embrace,
Laughter blooms in every space!

Shadows in Stitched Silence

In secret seams where shadows play,
Cotton giggles in a soft ballet.
A snicker hides in every fold,
Whispers daring, tales retold!

A shadow here, a shadow there,
Boldly winking, without a care.
With needle's prance, they plot and scheme,
In this silent frolic, they let off steam!

Stitches knot with playful flair,
Creating mischief, oh so rare.
A seamstress grins, her secrets bare,
In this fabric world, who wouldn't dare?

Lurking threads in twilight's hue,
Laughing softly as they construe.
Bound together, fun as fate,
In their whimsical, stitched crate!

The Dance of Delicate Twine

Ribboned footsteps on the floor,
They twirl and sway, a fancy score.
With each twist, a giggle's spun,
In this grand dance, they've just begun!

A tangle here, a knot up high,
Who knew strings could laugh and fly?
With playful leaps and heart-shaped pirouettes,
This cheeky twirl, they won't forget!

Chasing threads through dim-lit halls,
They waltz 'til laughter freely falls.
With taffeta dreams and joy alive,
In this silly dance, they all thrive!

So join the fun and don't restrain,
With whimsical patterns, lose the mundane.
United in threads, they shimmy and shine,
For in this frolic, all is divine!

The Richness of Touch

Fingers dance like butterflies,
On treasures wrapped in sly disguise.
A nudge, a wink, a playful tease,
What's hidden here? Just take a peek!

In rooms adorned with whispers shared,
Each fiber holds a secret dared.
Like tickles on an unsuspecting knee,
The thrill of touch sets laughter free.

An accidental brush, a startled shout,
What's this about? A curious route.
The fabric giggles, teasing so,
A joyful echo we all know!

Let's play with threads, entwine our quest,
For every clasp, a playful jest.
In silly games, old charms resound,
With each soft stroke, new laughs abound!

Elegant Chains and Sultry Veils

Shiny things that jingle bright,
They dangle heavy in the light.
With every step, they clink and clatter,
Creating chaos, laughter's matter.

Veils that tease and slightly hide,
A peek-a-boo, a giddy ride.
What's beneath this mystery?
A jest concealed, a giggle spree.

Chains that bind yet set us free,
A paradox of glee, you see?
With every tug, a silly game,
A playful dance, no hint of shame.

Twists and turns, oh what a sight!
Each clasp a nod to sheer delight.
In this riddle of fabric fun,
Let's frolic till the day is done!

Hidden Narratives in Softness

Soft touches whisper tales untold,
Like bedtime stories, warm and bold.
A gentle poke, a squeaky laugh,
In folds and curls, a playful path.

Every stitch a rib-tickling line,
Woven winks and hints divine.
The tales they tell, oh what a ride,
In quiet corners, joy can hide.

Feathers brush like secret words,
Crafting smiles without a verb.
In this gentle, silly dance,
Frolic with whimsy, not a chance!

So tie the knots of laughter's art,
Embrace the fun, let joy restart.
For every twist and playful sway,
Brings giggles bright to light the way!

The Poetry of Restraint

A knot that holds, yet frees the flame,
In playful binds, we stake our claim.
With tugs and pulls, we joyfully tease,
Laughter dances in every squeeze.

Surrendered whims, we dance on air,
A subtle game, a fanciful dare.
With every twist, a playful shout,
In the poetry of fun, we flout.

Most see only what's on display,
But here, my friend, we twist and sway.
Each gentle tug tells tales of thrill,
Let's laugh and play, we've time to kill!

So come and join this merry jest,
In quirky knots we find our rest.
With every rhyme, a giggle's spun,
In soft constraints, we find our fun!

Patterns of Daring Elegance

In a world of threads and schemes,
Patterns dance, or so it seems.
Stitch by stitch, with flair so bold,
Fashion tales that must be told.

Feathers here and spikes so low,
Strut the runway, steal the show.
Twirls and spins in quirky glee,
A wardrobe mishap, oh, the spree!

Bows and knots, all mismatched brains,
Who knew style could cause such strains?
Tango with the fabric's twist,
In the chaos, brush a fist!

A caper decked in polka dots,
Accents made of wild lots.
Waltzing light and hopping high,
We wear our quirks, and that's no lie!

The Tension of Finesse

Elegant strut in mismatched shoes,
With fashion bloopers, who can refuse?
A glance in the mirror, just one peek,
Oh dear, that outfit's at its peak!

Buttons popping, sequins sway,
Who knew style could go astray?
A clash of textures, bound to tease,
What a sight, it brings us ease.

Daring moves, a flip and spin,
Let's hope the seams hold us in!
A wink and a nod, with high flair,
What's laughter without a bit of dare?

Sashes tangled, a crazy quilt,
Bold choices made with no guilt.
With charm and chuckles, we prance
In the spotlight, we take our chance!

Twisted Dreams and Textures

In a closet where shadows play,
Cotton candy dreams in disarray.
Satin slips with slips of grace,
Who knew fashion could take place?

Twists and turns, oh how we bend,
Fabrics clash, but that's the trend.
Velvet whispers, shiny bold,
Make us giggle, never old.

A garter belt and polka spots,
Outfit tangled in wise thought.
Walking the line of silly flair,
Oops, this style is a nightmare!

A playful yarn, a frayed seam chance,
Outrageous fun in our dance.
Wear that mishap, wear it proud,
Laughter echoes through the crowd!

A Path Woven with Contrast

From quiet threads to boisterous seams,
We wander through our fabric dreams.
Colossal bows on tiny ties,
Watch out world, we're in for a surprise!

Odd colors clash, a sight to behold,
Gather 'round, let's break the mold.
Tangled strands of whimsy height,
Riding fashion's crazy flight.

A patchwork heart with noisy flair,
Style that shouts, without a care.
Swaying wildly, behold the show,
In this mishmash, watch us glow!

Zip and snap, snug and free,
Don't mind our clothes, just sing with glee.
For fabric fun, we'll take a bet,
In this chaos, no regrets!

Shimmering Edges and Rough Corners

In a world of glimmer and gleam,
Where corners poke and seams seem to scream,
They dance a jig, a silly affair,
With twirls and twists, they don't seem to care.

Frills and quirks in a jumbled heap,
A waltz of misfits, they tumble and leap,
One says, 'You're sharp!' while the other one pouts,
'You can't handle the curves!' they squabble and shout.

Straps loosely dangling, a humorous sight,
Like clumsy marionettes tangled in light,
Each step is a giggle, a jest on the floor,
As they stumble and tumble, laughing for more.

Edge to edge, and corner to edge,
In fashion's embrace, they forge a new pledge,
To wear all the threads that tickle and tease,
And dance through the night, fueled by mischief and cheese.

Entwined in Charcoal and Cream

Threaded in shadows, they bumble about,
A silly duo, filled with jest and doubt,
One's frothy with cream, the other so dark,
Together they spark, oh what a fine lark!

They giggle and jibe at each twist and turn,
Fashion's great folly, with lessons to learn,
She says, 'You're bold!' and he counters with flair,
'You can't match my style or my wild, crazy hair!'

Bound by mischief in shades of the night,
They flaunt what they've got, with giggles and light,
Tangled in layers that fumble and sway,
Making the mundane a humorous play.

So raise up a toast to this chaotic blend,
Where every misstep is a new tale to send,
In charcoal and cream, let the humor unfurl,
As they dance through the chaos, this mad, merry whirl.

Fabricated Desires

In a workshop of whimsy, dreams take their flight,
Stitching together some playful delight,
With patterns so wild, they prance off the reel,
Like a jester in motion, a comic appeal.

Those buttons that jingle, those zippers that squeak,
A chorus of laughter that hits just the peak,
One fabric complains, 'You don't fit the role!'
The other retorts, 'At least I have soul!'

Sewn with a smile and fraying at seams,
They tumble like puppets in whimsical dreams,
Each pull on the thread is a quirky embrace,
As they rattle and rumble, each testing new grace.

In a tapestry woven of giggles and fun,
Where nothing's quite perfect, yet all seems to run,
Fabricated desires, they spin and they play,
Crafting a world that's a laugh every day.

Tangles of Sweet Rebellion

In a closet of chaos, where styles collide,
Two rebels rejoice, with no place to hide,
Each piece is a story of topsy-turvy,
Designs so absurd, yet worn oh so curvy.

One says, 'Let's wear polka dots here and there!'
The other retorts, 'But what if it's rare?'
A mismatched ensemble of colors and dreams,
Oh, how they blend in their fanciful schemes!

Tangled and frayed, they laugh at the past,
With wrinkles and twists that forever will last,
The world can be rigid, they dance to their song,
Embracing each flaw, where the quirky belong.

Anarchy swirls in their fabrics, so bright,
They spin with abandon under moon's silver light,
For in tangled delight, they find their own way,
These sweet rebels of fashion, who play every day.

The Cloak of Intrigue

In shadows she dances, all dressed in delight,
Her outfit is winking, but it's hard to get right.
With zippers and buttons, she twists and she twirls,
Provoking a giggle from the boys and the girls.

The fabric is whispering secrets and dreams,
Each thread tells a story that pops at the seams.
A cape full of mischief, with flair and with fun,
She'll hide from the prying, on the run, on the run.

Worn with a grin, it defies all the norms,
A playful illusion that dances and swarms.
As laughter erupts in her captivating wake,
She revels in nonsense, make no mistake.

So here's to the garments that tickle and tease,
The sly little secrets that bend at the knees.
With every outfit, we step out of line,
In our playful attire, we're simply divine.

Emotions Bound in Fabric

In a riot of colors, the feelings emerge,
With patterns and prints that demand to converge.
An outfit for laughter, for grins and for cheer,
Where all of our secrets are strung up, oh dear!

Ties twisted, knotted, like the mind on a spree,
When wearing this madness, we're all fancy-free.
A jacket with laughter, a hat made of jokes,
We stumble through life like a bunch of old folks!

With sleeves full of giggles and pants lined with fun,
Each moment's a fashion, a game to be won.
Our hearts are like pockets, both heavy and light,
In garments of joy, everything feels right.

So wear your emotions in shades that are bright,
Be bold in your choices, let's laugh through the night.
For fabric and folly together entwined,
Bring humor and warmth, leaving worries behind.

Textured Memories

The quilt of our past is made with a smile,
Each patch tells a story, a whimsical style.
A funky old sweater with holes in the seams,
It carries my laughter, my hopes, and my dreams.

Remember that tutu from years long ago?
I twirled like a fairy, in melodious flow.
Now it sits snugly, on a mannequin bright,
A relic of joy from a magical night.

Those boots that I wore when I danced in the rain,
Still hold all my twirls, and a touch of my pain.
Each scuff tells a tale of adventures so sweet,
A testament lived in my worn-out retreat.

So here's to the textures that fashion our lore,
In vibrant and funky, in plaid or in score.
For memories tangled in fabric so fine,
Become the laughter that forever will shine.

Ties that Bind

With ribbons and bows that knot up my day,
It's hard not to giggle as I prance on my way.
A belt's tight embrace feels like a playful hug,
While mismatched socks give my outfit a shrug.

Each string pulls my joy in a curious dance,
I stumble and tumble, yet still take a chance.
In garments that twinkle, I step out with flair,
With ties that unfasten the tension in air.

Like shoelaces flapping, I chase after dreams,
Each pair tells a joke, or so it seems.
At times I'm a mess, yet I wear it with pride,
In the ties that connect us, I gladly confide.

So let's knot up our laughter and wear it around,
In threads of delight, the joy can be found.
For life's funny fabric is stitched with a grin,
And the ties that we make only deepen the spin.

Veils of Intrigue

In the corner, a mystery sits,
Draped in a playful kind of wit.
Whispers float, a teasing game,
Every glance feels just the same.

Patterns twist, they dance around,
A giggle's echo, a silly sound.
What's hidden? Oh, who could guess?
Unraveling is quite a mess!

Capes of charm and cheeky cheer,
In the chaos, I persevere.
Dare I peek beneath the folds?
Curiosity strikes, behold!

In this realm of cheeky tease,
I tiptoe with the greatest ease.
Each layer more absurdly bright,
A laugh, a glance, into the night.

Tangles of Touch

A twirl, a spin, oh what a plight,
Caught in a fabric's playful bite.
Fingers slip, and giggles flare,
Tangled stories fill the air.

Textured whispers, oh what fun,
Playing hide and seek, we run.
Soft and rough, a silly game,
Each touch exotic, none the same.

Threads entwined, we blur the lines,
With every twist, the laughter shines.
Knots unravel, hearts collide,
In this chaos, we can't hide.

Fabric fly, let's share the jest,
In this tangle, we're truly blessed.
Each smile woven, a joyous clutch,
A whirlwind dance, a silly touch.

The Allure of Depth

In shadows where the secrets coil,
Beneath the surface, we all toil.
A peek inside, a playful dive,
What strange treasures come alive?

Layers whisper, mysteries tease,
With every glance, bring me to my knees.
Oh what lies in the folds so steep?
The laughter's rich, it runs so deep.

Wonders bloom and quirky tones,
In every crevice, a giggle groans.
With every depth, a snicker found,
In this rabbit hole, joy abounds!

Curiosity leads me near,
To unearth what's brimming here.
In tangled fun and gentle stealth,
I dive right in for all my wealth.

Fire and Fabric

Dancing flames in a playful glow,
Wrapped in colors, a vibrant show.
The heat, it sizzles with every thread,
Where mischief teases, laughter's bred.

Beneath the heat, the stories sway,
Fabrics shimmer, come out to play.
A flicker here, a spark of glee,
In this chaos, we're wild and free.

Textures merge in a blazing cheer,
Every stitch whispers, "Come draw near!"
With every twist, the warmth sets in,
A cozy hug that makes me grin.

So let the fire dance and twirl,
With whimsy wrapped in every swirl.
This laughter burns, with every flare,
In the warmth of joy, we all share.

Moonlit Textiles

Under the glow of playful beams,
Stitching dreams with silly seams,
A thread of laughter, soft and bright,
Dancing shadows in the night.

Whimsical patterns, twirls and swirls,
Ticklish fabrics making you twirl,
Each fabric whispering cheeky truths,
In this world of vibrant spoofs.

A tapestry knotted with giggles loud,
Worn like crowns, we feel so proud,
With every stitch, a joke unfolds,
Stories of mischief humorously told.

In this realm of fibers so dear,
We twine our laughter, share our cheer,
For beneath each fold and every thread,
A tapestry of joy is made and spread.

The Tactile Journey

Tug on the corners, feel the jest,
Textures colliding, put to the test,
A tickle here, a pat just there,
Taking nudges, without a care.

Fluffy fluff and wiggly bits,
Make us laugh, it never quits,
The softer side, a fuzzy game,
Who knew fabric could bring such fame?

Slipping, sliding with brand-new friends,
On this journey, fun never ends,
We race through piles of fabric stacks,
Giggling wildly at silly knickknacks.

With each new touch, a grin appears,
As textures play with hopes and fears,
Let's roll in this tactile delight,
And smile together through the night.

Sculpted Sentiments

Sewn with care, peculiar charms,
Hugging heartstrings, with open arms,
Doodles etched on every seam,
Fabrics that conspire and scheme.

Twisting frills with a wink and nod,
A quirky quilt where thoughts are flawed,
Each patch a giggle, a soft embrace,
In a whimsical and happy place.

Like a card from a friend, cozy and warm,
These sentiments crafted, a playful charm,
Laughter trapped in every fold,
Wrapped in joy, a story told.

So here we stand, with fabric's care,
Creating magic in the air,
With sculpted whispers, we find our song,
In the quirkiest of hearts, we all belong.

Swathed in Mystery

Wrapped in giggles, a charming riddle,
Confetti threads twirl, playing fiddle,
Mysteries formed in quirky hues,
Tales of laughter hiding in views.

What's beneath the layers of fun?
A treasure hunt where all are one,
Textures play hide and seek with glee,
In this cozy cryptic jubilee.

Peek through openings, catch a glimpse,
Of zany adventures in playful limps,
Surprise encounters, and puns galore,
Wrapped in fabric they simply adore.

A shroud of giggles, so much to share,
In this fun-filled world, we declare,
Mysteries waiting, twirls on the floor,
In the embrace of fun, forevermore.

Fabricated Fantasies

In a world of whimsy, fabric dreams unwind,
Tangled threads of laughter, humor intertwined.
A corset of giggles, a belt of delight,
Strapped in with fun, we dance through the night.

With zippers of joy, and pockets of jest,
We fashion our folly, it's truly the best.
Patchwork of pranks, a quilt of fun,
Every stitch a smile, in the light of the sun.

Frills and thrills, a frolicsome spree,
In this fabric of joy, there's room for the free.
No serious worries, just whimsical threads,
As we weave through the worries, and laugh off the dreads.

So gather your friends, in costumes so bright,
With patterns of humor, let's take flight.
In our joyous creation, let laughter be sewn,
For fabric fantasies can never be overblown.

Embracing the Duality

In the realm of contrasts, we play with delight,
A zipper of laughter, a buckle so tight.
Soft whispers of mischief, and the roar of the bold,
In shades of the funny, our stories unfold.

A tie that binds us, yet lets us be free,
Where the wild meets the tame, is the place we agree.
With a wink and a nod, fashion's own jest,
Combining the playful with what we love best.

Two sides of a coin, like a heart in disguise,
We dance through the fabric, with mischief in our eyes.
Embracing the silly, the strange and the fun,
Together we giggle, united as one.

In outfits unique, we strut with great glee,
Twisting tradition, just you wait and see.
For the duality's charm, in giggles we trust,
In playful attire, nothing's a must.

Stitching Together Souls

In a workshop of laughter, we gather to play,
With needles of joy, we stitch the day away.
Binding our hearts with threads of the bright,
Creating connections, oh what a delight!

A patch here and there, with a dash of good cheer,
Every quilted moment, we hold dear.
Sewing our secrets, in patterns so swell,
With a twinkle in our eyes, we weave our own spell.

From caps of mischief to socks piled high,
In this crafting of souls, we let out a sigh.
The fabric of friendship is warm to the touch,
In this stitching of hearts, we've gained so much.

So gather your canvas, let's color the scene,
In hues of hilarity, where we've always been.
With laughter our needle, and joy our spool,
We're stitching together, like laughter's own rule.

Knotting the Heartstrings

In a playful tangle, our heartstrings entwine,
With knots of hilarity, oh so divine.
A dance of absurdity, with a wink and a grin,
In the fabric of friendship, where laughter begins.

When we tie up the jokes, in ribbons of cheer,
Every twist a memory, delightful and dear.
Laces may bind us, but laughing is free,
In jokingly knotted, imperfect esprit.

And with each little tug, our spirits ignite,
Bright colors of humor, they shine through the night.
Hearts woven together in messy delight,
With yarns of affection, our joy is in sight.

So let's fasten the laughter, embrace every thread,
In the tapestry of friendship that keeps us well-fed.
With smiles as the glue, and jokes as the seam,
We knotted our heartstrings, living the dream.

Imagined Embraces

In a room full of ruffles, they spun and twirled,
With winks and smirks, prancing like girls.
Satin so shiny, it gleamed like the sun,
They laughed at the thought of a race that's begun.

Faux fur and twine, the chaos was neat,
Every stitched seam kept them light on their feet.
A tussle of high heels, a grand dizzy dance,
Oh, the folly of missteps, who said they had chance?

Giggling echoes, their antics were bold,
A strap that kept slipping, too daring to hold.
They fancied themselves in a dramatic farce,
Until one fell over—a slip, oh so sparse!

With laughter erupting, the party took flight,
As pants and skirts tangled through the starlit night.
In every bizarre whirl and jump that they made,
Fun was the fabric they couldn't evade.

The Stitching of Secrets

Behind a closed door, they whisper and scheme,
Admiring the frills like a curious dream.
With needles and threads, they plotted with glee,
What secrets could hide in a capricious spree?

A giggle erupted at one crafty thought,
A slip of the tongue, a scandalous plot.
The socks and suspenders had stories to tell,
Of clumsy encounters and mishaps as well.

With pins and with patterns, they crafted their fate,
From the sweetest of dreams to the wildest of state.
Each twirl of fabric pronounced a new joke,
As they hastily stitched every burst, every poke.

In layers of mirth, they wrapped every tease,
Conspirators hidden in patches and pleats.
For friendships were woven in cheeky delight,
As they stitched every secret beneath the starlight.

Whispers Beneath the Fabric

Beneath quirky layers, soft whispers abound,
Of bold dreams and blunders, laughter unbound.
Silk ribbons flutter, secrets flit near,
Daring little giggles danced on the clear.

The snags and the threads, an unlikely affair,
Yet stitching them close was an absolute dare.
What joy packed in pockets, what tales on the seam,
In a wild burst of colors they dared to dream.

Loud patterns shouted while whispers would creep,
As they plotted together, cutting corners so steep.
Each piece spun a story that tickled the bone,
With cracks of delight that they gleefully sown.

Underneath all the garb, hilarity dwells,
An embroidery of laughter that fits like a spell.
So next time you ponder the humor of dress,
Remember the whispers, and outlandish finesse.

The Richness of Contrast

Stark black against white—what a sight to behold,
In a cackle of contrasts, the stories unfold.
Dare little patches, both fierce and demure,
Could lead to a moment both quirky and pure.

Frayed edges of laughter, an unexpected thrill,
Caught between frivolity, highbrow, and chill.
Ballet of colors, a flamboyant embrace,
Where awkward meets elegance—a wild chase.

The texture of humor, so rich and so bold,
Embracing oddities, breaking the mold.
From wild mismatched socks to a whimsically neat,
Every layer and nuance makes life feel complete.

In contrasts of life, comedy thrives,
In garments as playful as the joy in our vibes.
So mix up your style, let surprises parade,
For the richness of laughter cannot be delayed.

The Texture of Desire

In shadows where secrets play,
Soft threads dance, come what may.
Stitching quirks with every glance,
Fingers fumble in the chance.

Woven whims in tangled schemes,
Giggling at our wildest dreams.
A tapestry of blushing hues,
Who knew textures could amuse?

Illusions of Strength

Strutting bold with puffed-up chest,
Behind the guise, a feeble jest.
Muscles flexed but laughter leaks,
A strong facade that simply squeaks.

Beneath the armor, giggles flare,
Chasing bravado in midair.
Foolish whims beneath the skin,
Strength is where the fun begins.

Twisted Ties

Knots binding tight, yet hearts unwind,
Jokes flow free, no need to mind.
A rope of banter, oh what a scene,
Giggles spill like soda keen.

With playful pulls and friendly shoves,
Each twist reveals what laughter loves.
Binding joy with every tease,
In playful knots, we find our ease.

Silhouette Dreams

In dim light, shapes start to prance,
Silhouettes waltz in a comical dance.
Shadowed figures, grins so wide,
In dreams of mischief, we just glide.

Chasing phantoms with a shout,
Twisted tales, we're all about.
No need for props, just fun that gleams,
Life's a joke beneath our dreams.

Enigmas in Each Weave

In the twist of threads so fine,
I pondered where they'd intertwine.
A puzzle wrapped in velvet hue,
Is it art or is it blue?

Twists and knots, a tangled mess,
My mind spins with sheer finesse.
If fashion's clues are riddles bold,
Then is confusion made of gold?

With every loop, a giggle grows,
What's the secret? Nobody knows!
I tiptoe through this fabric maze,
In a wild dance, I lose the craze.

The patterns shift with playful cheer,
Whispers hint at things unclear.
Oh dear fabric, you tease so well,
A game of threads, a woven spell!

Sultry Intersections

Two paths collide with cheeky flair,
One feels daring, one is rare.
Caught between with a wink and grin,
Which one's trouble? Where to begin?

A mix of spice with sweet surprise,
A peek-a-boo, oh, how time flies!
This rendezvous, beautifully bold,
Is it chance or fate retold?

Beneath the surface, sparks escalate,
Each secret glance, a twist of fate.
With every laugh, the tension grows,
Who knew this dance would leave us foes?

In tangled steps, we find our groove,
An intersection we dare to move.
With playful hearts and mischief's grace,
We fumble in this secret space!

The Interplay of Shadow and Light

In shadows cast by colors bright,
A playful jest, a laugh in sight.
The glimmer whispers mischief's tune,
As day's delight turns into moon.

A twirl of dusk with cheeky tease,
Illusions swirl upon the breeze.
Which way to step in this jesting show?
Find balance, or watch your toe!

Where light will flirt and shadows play,
A game of hide-and-seek today.
Laughter dances on the seams,
While daydreamers spin their themes.

The contrast sings of fun in flight,
A wild waltz with hearts alight.
Oh, this duel of dark and bright,
Together we laugh into the night!

Silken Bonds

Tangled threads of friendly ties,
In every knot, a few sweet lies.
We wrap ourselves in laughter's flair,
With playful hearts, we shed our care.

In silky strands, our secrets weave,
A touch of mischief up our sleeve.
With every pull, a giggle grows,
This snug embrace, it always shows!

As bonds entwine, we beam with glee,
What silly things will we decree?
With every twist, a story spun,
In tangled joy, we laugh as one.

With gentle tug and playful tease,
These silken ties put us at ease.
In this embrace, confusion's fine,
So here's to fun, a friendship's spine!

The Harmony of Opposites

In a world where light meets dark,
A frolicsome spark, a playful lark.
One's dressed in silence, the other in sound,
Dancing together, beautifully unbound.

The studded boots stomp, the satin glides,
With giggles and wiggles, the silliness rides.
One steals the stage, the other the show,
Who knew that chaos could twirl so slow?

A tie-dye heart and a sturdy resolve,
In this quirky dance, all problems absolve.
They twist and they twirl, a mismatched duet,
In the end, who knows, they may not regret.

So here's to the play of contrasts that tease,
A jester's laughter, a dignified sneeze.
Revel in oddities, let spirits take flight,
Together they shine, day into night.

Threads of Enchantment

A twinkle of mischief, a swirl of delight,
Threading through moments, oh what a sight!
With a wink and a nod, the fabric does shine,
Tangled together, your fumble with mine.

The silver bells jingle, a tangle ensues,
With playful missteps, we dance in our shoes.
A stitch in the belly, laughter in tow,
Who knew that fun had a crafting flow?

Join in the chaos, let patterns collide,
A seamstress of silliness, dance the wild ride.
With scissors in hand, we trim off the fray,
Creating a masterpiece, come what may!

So raise up your glass to the threads that we weave,
For each knot and each loop is a trick up our sleeve.
Mirth in the fabric, joy in the threads,
Woven together, where whimsy treads.

Woven Destinies

In the loom of laughter, our fates intertwine,
Each fiber a joke, each thread a punchline.
Twirling through mishaps, we stumble and slide,
Our destiny woven, a raucous ride.

A tapestry vibrant, with stories and pranks,
A color parade, we join in the ranks.
From golden to teal, each shade brings a grin,
For every misfortune, we find a win!

Knots of surprise in a fabric so free,
With every blunder, we giggle with glee.
So here's to the chaos, the quirks and the play,
In this woven adventure, let's jive all the way!

So tiptoe through stitches, leap through the fun,
With each little twist, we laugh as we run.
Woven together, our tales never cease,
For joy is the thread that will never be leased.

Gossamer Hues

In shadows that shimmer, in whispers that sing,
A frothy parade of the lightest of things.
Soft giggles entwined, like clouds in the sky,
A feathery jest, oh my, oh my!

A splash of pink, a dab of bright blue,
With swirls of illusion, this party's a zoo!
The lightest of breezes blows tickles our cheeks,
With colorful patterns, we giggle and peek.

With wisps of confusion, we float on a dream,
Here in this frolicsome, playful regime.
A carnival laughter, a whimsical breeze,
With gossamer shades, let's party with ease!

So dance in the dappled, jester's delight,
For in every chuckle, our spirits take flight.
We're draped in the joy of the softest of hues,
In this raucous tapestry, let's weave every muse.

www.ingramcontent.com/pod-product-compliance
Lightning Source LLC
Chambersburg PA
CBHW060111230426
43661CB00003B/148